TRUCKS

TRANSPORTATION

David and Patricia Armentrout

Rourke
Publishing LLC
Vero Beach, Florida 32964

www.rourkepublishing.com

PHOTO CREDITS: ©DigitalVision, LLC Cover, pp. 4, 21; ©Armentrout p. 8; ©Publishers Image Resource p. 15; ©Freightliner Title, p.18; ©Volvo pp. 7, 10, 13, 17.

Title page: *The extra space behind the driver's seat is called a sleeper.*

Editor: Frank Sloan

Cover design by Nicola Stratford

Library of Congress Cataloging-in-Publication Data

Armentrout, David, 1962-
  Trucks / David and Patricia Armentrout.
      p. cm. — (Transportation)
Includes bibliographical references and index.
Contents: Transport — Land transport — A popular system of transport
—Big rig tractors — Big rig trailers — Auto transporters — Tank
trucks — Buses are trucks too! — Trucks at work — Dates to remember.
  ISBN 1-58952-673-2 (hardcover)
  1. Trucks—Juvenile literature. [1. Trucks.] I. Armentrout, Patricia,
1960- II. Title. III. Series: Armentrout, David, 1962-
Transportation.

TL230.15.A73 2003
629.224--dc21
                                                              2003007277

Printed in the USA

CG/CG

Table of Contents

Transport

Transportation is a system of moving people or cargo from one place to another. Our modern world has many kinds of transportation. One of the most familiar is truck transport. Trucks are very important to our **economy**. Trucks of all kinds move cargo over millions of miles of roads and highways. Take a look around your house or school. Almost everything you see was probably delivered in a truck.

Seen from the air, highway systems can look like a maze.

Land Transport

The first overland cargo carriers were **domesticated** animals such as dogs, camels, goats, and horses. Cargo was strapped to their backs or pulled in sleds or wagons. Locomotives were the next great step in land transport.

However, the invention of the gasoline-powered **internal combustion** automobile in 1885 changed everything. Internal combustion engines made the use of small, self-propelled vehicles practical.

Internal combustion engines were quickly put to use in automobiles and trucks.

A Popular System of Transport

Gasoline-powered trucks became common in the early 1900s. Their popularity continued to grow as more roads and highways were added. By 1918, more than one million trucks were in use in the United States. By 2000, more than 80 million trucks and buses of all sizes were transporting people and cargo across the country. Today, it's nearly impossible to drive on a highway without seeing a truck at work.

Cranes are used to transfer cargo containers from railcars to truck trailers.

9

Big Rig Tractors

Big rigs, or tractor-trailers, are the biggest trucks on the road. Big rigs have two parts. The first part is the tractor. The tractor has a powerful engine and a cab. Most modern tractors are powered by diesel fuel rather than gasoline. The cab is where the driver sits. Some cabs also have sleepers behind the driver. A sleeper cab has room for the driver to relax or sleep when not driving. The tractor pulls, or tows, the second part—the trailer.

A sleeper compartment is a truck driver's office on wheels.

Big Rig Trailers

A big rig's trailer holds the cargo. Trailers are sometimes called semi-trailers because they only have rear wheels. The front end is supported by the tractor. There are many types of semi-trailers. Some trailers are enclosed and can hold anything from boxes of fruit to furniture. Other trailers are open and have flatbeds. Flatbed trailers can haul heavy equipment up to 30 tons (27 metric tons).

Big rigs are sometimes called 18-wheelers.

Auto Transporters

An auto transporter is another kind of trailer. Auto transporters carry cars. Cars are driven one after another, up a ramp onto the trailer. The cars are then strapped into place so they won't fall off. Auto transporters can haul eight or more cars at once.

14

Auto transporters carry vehicles from the manufacturer to the dealership.

Tank Trunks

Many products cannot be carried in standard semi-trailers. In some cases specially designed trailers must be used. Tank, or **tanker**, trucks are built to carry liquids. There are many kinds of tanker trucks. Chemicals, gas, oil, water, and milk are some of the products that are transported by tanker trucks.

A tanker is loaded with oil at the refinery.

Buses Are Trucks Too!

Have you ever taken a ride in a big truck? Thousands of kids ride in a type of truck almost every day. You have probably guessed what type of truck they ride in—a school bus. Buses are trucks that are built to carry passengers. Some passenger buses have plush seats, televisions, and even a bathroom. Don't you wish school buses were built that way?

School buses are trucks that provide transportation for millions of children.

19

Trucks at Work

The next time you travel on a highway, look for the many kinds of trucks and trailers that use our roads. You will likely see vans called panel trucks used for deliveries. You may see giant dump trucks that haul dirt. Cement trucks, tow trucks, moving vans, and snowplows also share the roads we use every day. You will begin to understand why we depend on trucks to keep our economy moving.

Snowplows clear our roads and haul salt for melting ice and snow.

Dates to Remember

1885	Gasoline-powered internal combustion automobile is invented
1896	First gas-powered truck
1900s	Gasoline-powered trucks become popular in the United States
1918	Number of trucks in use in the United States surpasses one million
1930s	First diesel-powered trucks are built
2000	Number of trucks in use in the United States surpasses 80 million

Glossary

domesticated (duh MESS tuh kayt ed) — animals that have been tamed by humans

economy (ee KON uh mee) — the way a country runs its industry, trade, and finance

internal combustion (in TUR nuhl kuhm BUSS chun) — an engine that burns fuel and air inside a combustion chamber

tanker (TANG kur) — a truck, ship, or airplane equipped with tanks for carrying liquids

Index

Further Reading

Francis, Dorothy. *Our Transportation Systems*. The Millbrook Press, 2002
Kilby, Don. *On the Road: Wheels at Work*. Kids Can Press, 2003
Stille, Darlene. *Big Rigs*. Compass Point Books, 2002

Websites To Visit

www.pacificnwtruckmuseum.org/index.html
www.enchantedlearning.com/themes/transportation.shtml
www.macktrucks.com/

About The Authors

David and Patricia Armentrout have written many nonfiction books for young readers on a variety of subjects. They have had several books published for primary school reading. The Armentrouts live in Cincinnati, Ohio, with their two children.